AF374160

Luminous Infusions

Wisdom to inspire self-awareness, discovery and empowering change

Beverly Brunelle

Published in the United States by: Beverly Brunelle
Photography: Beverly Brunelle
Layout & Cover Design: Mariah Miller Creative Services

ISBN: 979-8-9874359-0-8

www.BeverlyBrunelle.com

I dedicate these writings to humanity.

To love, appreciation, and compassion blossoming.

To deeply listening, feeling, and understanding.

To humility.

To wisdom flourishing.

To new creative possibilities.

For ALL.

Table of Contents

Introduction

These inspiring messages are *Luminous Infusions* that can awaken consciousness to support more expansive experiences of yourself, your relations and the world. These are tools for shifting your realities into greater possibilities for empowering change. The messages can inspire you to access your deeper wisdom, creativity and authentic presence. New perspectives can be born that create new healthy dynamics in relationships.

We are all first in relationship with ourselves. To be present with others, we must first be present and honest with ourselves. Our inner dialogue, perceptions, beliefs, cultural and ancestral influences, and how we treat ourselves, these all shape our ways of relating.

Luminous Infusions are a phenomenal resource for shifting consciousness. LI supports us moving from unconscious habits of repeating family, social and cultural conditioning into more self-honesty and inner freedom to consciously create new possibilities. LI is a guide for self-intimacy, to know ourselves more deeply and clearly, and to be in relationship with others from this intimate place. LI support us to blossom in new enriching ways to create the relationships, life, and the world we are deeply craving.

We are all energy and awareness becoming awake to itself. *Luminous Infusions* is a result of a meditation practice inviting the highest guidance from pure creation to support humanity to live into and from our continuous awakening.

These writings are living wisdom, potent in simplicity and unique with every reading. May these passages encourage you, the reader, to align with your deep sacred Essence, intuition and wisdom. May you experience your authentic, passionate, unique aliveness continuing to blossom.

Enjoy the journey.

Beverly Brunelle

How to Use Luminous Infusions

To enjoy the blessings herein, breathe.

Tune in and ask yourself:

~ Are you willing to listen deeply to your inner knowing and intuition?

~ Are you willing to explore new possibilities, receive new insights and take new inspired action with ease, grace, love and joy?

~ What particular personal situation do you want to explore through *Luminous Infusions*?

Request: clarity, insight and deeper inner knowing.

Clarify your intention. Ask your question.

Open the book spontaneously. Read the quote before you.

Notice how the words resonate. What new insights, perceptions, visions, and guidance comes forth for you?

Hold the book in your hands, or if digital, intend and welcome the perfect message and the highest insights it inspires for you at this time. Be clear with your intention. Flip, or if it is an ebook, scroll through the book or table of contents and organically stop on a message. Or simply open the book to the message that shows up.

Relax, your mind, expectations and any preconceived assumptions. Be open to new possibilities as you read the passage(s) Tune into your intuition. Notice the sensations in your body and your senses. What impulse and insights come to you? What pictures come up, what thoughts? How does this passage relate to your situation?

The purpose of the Inquiry Practice is to stimulate deeper self-discovery.

It is important to allow your inner wisdom to reveal itself to you. Wondering how the passage is relevant to your situation will open opportunities to discover new perspectives and ways of being. If you want more clarification of the response you have received, ask specifically for that and pick another passage.

As you read, notice shifts in your perspectives, new insights and your body's response. You are your own best resource. You can work with a new message each day or each week as a guide to inspire authentic change.

Play with creating questions that will open new possibilities: "What is important for me to know? How can I bring more love and clarity into this situation? What will create a quantum shift in my consciousness? What is in alignment with my greater well-being? What will help me move forward with greater honesty and ease, honoring everyone involved? What is my highest action in this situation? How can I allow my Essence to come through more easily?"

Read the messages from a place of contemplation. Remember to breathe . . . relax . . . be curious. Appreciate your willingness to learn about yourself and to create a new world of experience and possibility for all.

Enjoy the inner exploration!

Beverly Brunelle

Acknowledge Yourself

1

Acknowledge Yourself

It is so important to acknowledge yourself: all feelings, longings and desires. It is the acknowledgement, without expectation, story attachment, or controlled response, that allows and frees the energy to be a creative force for all good.

Inquiry Practice

What feelings, longings and desires can you acknowledge more honestly to yourself? What is their deeper message for you? Journal this inquiry daily for your own self-discovery. Use what you learn to inform new perspectives, communications and actions.

Beverly Brunelle

Align with Your Awakening

2

Align with Your Awakening

Find new ways to communicate that support you, and those involved, to thrive on life and creative possibilities. Be aware of your energy as you feel depleted and as you feel enlivened. Make choices that are in alignment with your awakening.

Inquiry Practice

Take a few deep breaths. Tune into what is more true for you. What do you need in this moment? What supports you in being more deeply honest in your communications?

Allow Essence to Move Through You

3

Allow Essence to Move Through You

The deepest surrender is in letting go of everything the mind challenges to keep in a specific order and in a specific framework. It is not irresponsible to give yourself inner space to let go and be available to an infusion of creative flow. Letting go is truly allowing Essence to move through you and to you in new ways and new channels. Let go. Invite and allow your Essence to flow through you.

Inquiry Practice

Take a few breaths. Relax mental tension. Let go of expectations. Ask: What does my Essence want me to know about the situation at hand? Invite new possibilities even if there seemingly are none. Notice what insights come to you.

Beverly Brunelle

Allow Freedom

4

Allow Freedom

Give up your absolute conditions of how the future and how others must be in order that you may thrive. The more you allow others their freedom, the more you allow yourself yours. The more you live your freedom, the more the world expands into new possibilities of satisfaction and fulfillment.

Inquiry Practice

Where are you allowing others to control you? Where are you trying to control others? Call your energy home from these situations and people. Notice how you feel. Why did you need to control? Why did you give in to others expectations? What new perspectives are available to you with the freedom of an open mind?

Beverly Brunelle

Allow Yourself Peace

5

Allow Yourself Peace

Allow yourself the peace that comes from honoring your Self. Take the rist to truly know yourself. Come from this place in your awareness, communications, and actions.

Inquiry Practice

Notice when you are not truthful with yourself. Notice when you withhold your truth from others. How and where can you honor your unique self more? Practice expressing your truth with yourself. Practice respectfully sharing your truth with others. Notice how you feel and how this practice influences your relationship dynamics.

Beverly Brunelle

All Senses Awake

6

All Senses Awake

Look at what you are creating and be honest with yourself. Ears open, eyes open, mind open, clear knowing. Be curious with all senses awake to the new and ever-changing.

Inquiry Practice

Truly listen to what you say and notice what you are calling into your experience. What do you want to change? If you are more honest with yourself, what new possibilities would you like to call into your experience? Choose words and communication that supports this.

Beverly Brunelle

Ask Yourself

7

Ask Yourself

"How is it that I become diverted from my own true path?"
Ask yourself this question with great regularity and you
will gain awareness and understanding to be more true to
yourself.

Inquiry Practice

What is your true path? In what ways do you distract
yourself, or hold yourself back, or devalue your intentions?
What supports you to be more on purpose? How can you
integrate your life purpose more fully into your everyday
actions and relations?

Beverly Brunelle

Become Your Heart's Desire

8

Become Your Heart's Desire

Nothing is too great to achieve. Dare to dream big beyond all seeming possibility. Become your heart's desire. All is possible with the Divinity within YOU.

Inquiry Practice

What are your secret heart's desires? Where do your heart's desires crave more freedom? Ask for support and commune often with your inner inspired genius and with your Essence. Gather support from friends, coaches, and the cosmos.

Beverly Brunelle

Be Free to Be Honest

9

Be Free to Be Honest

Let go of the perfect way to respond in any given moment. Let yourself come from deep within. The closer you get in touch with your own wanting and your own body, the more free and honest you will become in every moment.

Inquiry Practice

You matter. If you were more honest with yourself, what would you let yourself know? Ask your inner wisdom: What do I really want and need? What am I hiding? Where do I need more freedom? More structure? Where can I be more honest with myself?

Beverly Brunelle

Be In Tune with Yourself

10

Be In Tune with Yourself

You have a responsibility to yourself, to life, and to creation, to not succumb to others feelings and desires unless they resonate with your own. To be truly in tune with yourself, that is the mystical spiritual journey. How you live it out is your own decision.

Inquiry Practice

Where do you lean into other people's expectations, judgments, and desires, and give up how you truly feel or what you want? Are you trying to belong, to fit in, to be liked, to be accepted, or to not rock the boat? Where can you trust your own desires and needs more? Be curious in your exploration.

Beverly Brunelle

Be in Great Integrity

11

Be in Great Integrity

It is a time to be in great integrity with one's own awareness of self and others. It is a time to be very clear, very honest and very real.

Inquiry Practice

How can you up-level your self-honesty? How can you apply it in your relationships, work, and everyday living? Where have you overridden another's boundaries? Or your own? Is there someone in your life who needs extra TLC, appreciation or support? Is there a situation with an old friend where it feels like it is time to bridge the distance?

Beverly Brunelle

Be Nurtured by the Unknown

12

Be Nurtured by the Unknown

The Divine nurtures you within. It comes so freely. Go deep within. Strengthen your bonds to the unknown. Open up to it as your lover, and breathe.

Inquiry Practice

The unknown is pure creation and pure potential. How do you feel when you "don't know" something? Take a deep breath and relax into the spaciousness of the unknown. Invite clarity and new possibilities. Keep relaxing your breathing. Notice the authentic inspiration, images and insights that come organically. It may take time, be patient.

Beverly Brunelle

Be Vigilant to Synchronicities

13

Be Vigilant to Synchronicities

Be open, vigilant, and curious in your surroundings, so that life's gifts of Divine interactions and synchronicities will be received. Appreciate these surprises and how they enrich your life.

Inquiry Practice

What synchronicities surprised you this week? When did you have a feeling or an intuition that came true? What request did you make to life that was answered? Did it come in expected or unexpected ways? Journal your observations.

Beverly Brunelle

Be You for Your Own Sake

14

Be You for Your Own Sake

You may wonder, "Who cares who I truly am?" It is for you to care. It is not for others. Know and be yourself for your own sake, for yourself alone.

Inquiry Practice

What messages did you receive as a child that denied your uniqueness? How have you internalized these messages? Call in your younger selves from those times. Give them a new home in your heart with new messages of freedom, love and acceptance.

Be Your Best Friend

15

Be Your Best Friend

Be your own best guide. Train yourself to do what you truly desire. Relax in the knowing that your goals are taking you to those places, people and experiences that will truly nourish you and all involved.

Inquiry Practice

What messages did you receive in your early years that challenged your heart's desires? What family patterns unconsciously denied you love? Call all those younger selves home to your heart to be loved, accepted and safe. Dialogue with them to discover more of your early true joy and pleasure. As those younger selves open to receiving more love and acceptance, what changes do you notice within you?

Beverly Brunelle

Bring Courage to the Forefront

16

Bring Courage to the Forefront

Let the fires of passion sweep away the fear, to bring courage to the forefront. Allow passion to create the sacred space you can step into to follow your dreams. It is never too late to begin anew to freshen your heart.

Inquiry Practice

Where has fear kept you away from living your dreams? In an ideal world what would you love to do? Love to be? Love to explore? What aspects have you kept hidden in order to feel safe? What would you do differently if your inner passions were freed? Journal this inquiry.

Compassion is a Great Source of Love

17

Compassion is a Great Source of Love

Join the flow of the river of compassion and love that exists within you . . . that *is* you. There you shall feel the true blessings and tenderness of your heart.

Inquiry Practice

Ask your body, your emotions, your inner child, where they need and want loving compassion to flow more freely? Breathe and relax as you invite loving compassion to these tender places and ages within. Notice what happens. Be open to insights. Journal, draw, doodle, or dance to integrate the new energies.

Beverly Brunelle

Creation is at Your Service

18

Creation is at Your Service

Set your goals, set your intentions, and take action. The steps will present themselves. Do not worry. Do not succumb to old thoughts of confusion and depletion. Act as if the whole world and creation are at your service, are at your feet, and ready to serve.

Inquiry Practice

Relax your breathing, your brain, and any sense of struggling. Call all your energy home to yourself from sources of worry, fear and limitation. Invite life and your wisest self to guide and support your needs and desires in new ways. Journal and ask what next steps will honor and support you to move forward. Relax any expectations and be willing to discover something new.

Deepen Your Connection

19

Deepen Your Connection

It is a time of giving up that which no longer serves you. Open to the heart of trust. Give away the powers of the "shoulds" and "ought-tos." Open to the situation at hand. How do you want to feel? What action supports that? Feel what will create that. The time of being in the head is the old way. Being in the body is the new way, in the present.

Inquiry Practice

What "shoulds" and "ought-tos" are obvious influences in your sense of self? In your relationships? In your work? What message does your deeper inner self have for you that supports you to live more in the current of love and wisdom that is within you? What perspectives and choices would give you more freedom to be truly YOU? Journal your inquiry. Notice how these new possibilities feel in your body.

Beverly Brunelle

Desire to Thrive

20

Desire to Thrive

Honor your heartfelt desires. Be patient. Gently guide your focus to that which you are wanting and step into that dream.

Inquiry Practice

Journal to explore: In an ideal world, where you were totally free and your desire to thrive was exuberant, what heartfelt dreams would you bring to life? What new perspectives would support these possibilities? What wise changes could you make now that would move you in that creative direction?

Experience the Love that Is

21

Experience the Love that Is

The old ways of suffocating yourself from love were intended to keep you safe. Allow yourself the power of discernment. Trust your capacities to experience the love that is.

Inquiry Practice

Where do you automatically say "No" when you really would love to say "YES?" Notice when you automatically move away from receiving support and appreciation. Notice when you don't trust, or feel safe, or are in automatic response mode, with what is being offered. Journal to reveal the underlying beliefs and to get really honest with yourself. Ask: "In an ideal world where I am honestly discerning, how could I receive more authentic love?"

Express Your Truth

22

Express Your Truth

Rather than pointing out what is wrong, express what is more true. "I want to feel the love between us. I want to deepen our friendship. I want to deepen our sense of community with each other." Be brave enough to express your truth. You will find it will turn minds around. It will turn realities around.

Inquiry Practice

Ask yourself often: "What is more true for me? What is underneath the habits of questioning, judging, being disappointed, and being angry at life? What do I really want?" Journal your inner exploration.

Feel Inspired!

23

Feel Inspired!

Your duty is to feel inspired. Let that feeling be a clue. The days when you are full of wonder are life changing, bringing you to a new reality, with new possibilities. There is strength in the energy of a new reality, but old limiting energy may still be present. The old wants to be transformed. Welcome its transformation into the new current of creation.

Inquiry Practice

How do you resource inspiration? Journal the question: What is possible (in a specific area of interest) that has been outside my current awareness? Journal the inspired possibilities that you receive. At bedtime ask your inner wisdom to inspire you in dreamtime. Have your journal by the bed to record pearls of wisdom upon waking.

Beverly Brunelle

Gather Your Energy

Gather Your Energy

24

Gather Your Energy

There is no need to doubt. Doubting is in vain. Look to that which is glorious! When you hear yourself in doubt or worry, look up and take a deep breath. Gather your energy from the past. Look to what you are wanting and be that. Be that self you are craving and that you are clearly in the knowing of.

Inquiry Practice

Be bold with your self awareness. What are you clearly in the knowing of, that you have been holding yourself back from acknowledging, expressing or creating? What steps will move you into your desired future ~ today and this week?

Beverly Brunelle

Give Up Needing to Control

25

Give Up Needing to Control

Allow for flexibility and magic, now and in your future. Give up needing to control life. Allow space in your expectations for new possibilities to blossom.

Inquiry Practice

Where have you been trying to control the future? Take several deep breaths and give space to your perceptions and expectations. Be spontaneous with this new spaciousness in the unknown of pure potential. Invite magic, flexibility and new possibilities to infuse the new space and inform you.

Beverly Brunelle

Give Yourself Freedom to Thrive

26

Give Yourself Freedom to Thrive

Give up your absolutes of how others must be in order for you to thrive. Give up your absolute conditions of how you must be in order for you to thrive.

Inquiry Practice

Practice noticing expectations, assumptions, and judgments you have of others and of yourself. Take some deep breaths to relax your body and mind. Bring your attention to your need to feel safe. Give yourself the compassion, understanding, and freedom to receive new inspiration and possibilities, which allow you to thrive in new ways in the situation at hand.

GLOW ~ Care for Yourself

27

GLOW ~ Care for Yourself

Allow your body to glow from within with the knowingness and self-lovingness that is always there within you. Breathe into your heart space to ignite its glow and to nourish your whole being.

Inquiry Practice

What can you do right now to tune into the love and wisdom within you? What clear intention and action supports your inner glow to grow?

Heighten Your Awareness

28

Heighten Your Awareness

Ask to be aware, one step at a time. Listen to others' opinions and be true to yourself. Look at what is happening within yourself. Observe the fluctuations. Do not allow yourself to be off balance for too long.

Inquiry Practice

Notice and be honest with yourself, when you feel resistant or angry with other's opinions and points of view. Notice how your body sensations react. Bring your attention to your breath and invite a relaxation of tensions. Journal: "What is being triggered in me when I react to another's difference in perceptions?" See what insights are revealed while you write.

Beverly Brunelle

Honestly Listen Within

29

Honestly Listen Within

It is necessary to listen within for your deeper, honest answers. Listening is a great skill. Listening to yourself is even a greater skill. There are many moments when you are trying to define yourself by those things around you: people, thoughts, beliefs, ways of being and functioning. Listen honestly within to the deeper truths of your being.

Inquiry Practice

You are a magnificent resource. Meditate and journal on these questions: "What is my deepest truth wanting me to know? What secrets am I keeping from myself? What strengths am I denying? What capacities and skills are important for me to develop?"

Beverly Brunelle

Honor Your Body

30

Honor Your Body

The sensuous, sacred, and erotic are all part of the disarming or un-armoring of the psyche. Honoring the body is a sacred entrance into the experience of the body divine.

Inquiry Practice

How can you honor your body more each day? What does your body need and want? What beliefs are in the way of you allowing yourself to experience and explore your subtle senses more? What can you do to give yourself a deepening experience of your body? Ask your body how it would like you to explore your sacred, sensuous and erotic self.

Beverly Brunelle

Honor Yourself More

31

Honor Yourself More

Many of your moments of unhappiness are due to a lack of honoring yourself. The more you honor yourself, the more you will live aligned with your authentic Essence. You will, then, be doing the things that you enjoy doing and being with the people you enjoy being with.

Inquiry Practice

It will be revealing to remember a time when you were unhappy. Ask your authentic Essence: "How could I have honored myself more? What did I really need?" Relax your expectations and be curious to learn about your deeper truths and possibilities. Practice this inquiry in the midst of future situations.

Beverly Brunelle

Just Be Open

32

Just Be Open

Many opportunities can come in the back door of experience, through unexpected channels. Just be open to the people and the places that surround you wherever you go and wherever you are. Be without judgment and without expectation. Just be open to what presents itself.

Inquiry Practice

Are you willing to allow the complexities of life to gift you with new delightful opportunities? Are you willing to be curious about how the mystery of life is going to delight you this day, in this meeting, in this experience, etc.? Are you willing to learn what is outside of your knowing? Make your intention, go forth and explore!

Beverly Brunelle

Leave Space for Grace

33

Leave Space for Grace

Follow through on your tasks, leaving space for grace to weave its way through the magic tapestry of your existence. You are not alone. Remember your power to invite the mystery to reveal new possibilities.

Inquiry Practice

Are you willing to be curious about what is outside of your knowing? Are you willing to receive support, inspiration, and something new from life? Are you willing to be surprised? Invite the energies of grace in and explore the possibilities.

Let Every Moment Be a Mystery

34

Let Every Moment Be a Mystery

Practice letting go of that which you hold on to, of that which you label others to be, whether it be your wanting of them or your observation of them. Just let it all go. Let every moment be a mystery to be revealed.

Inquiry Practice

Breathe. Practice the above. Ask: Are you willing to be in the mystery of life? Notice who you have been judging and reacting to. Relax your mind and bring your attention to your breathing. Call your energy home to yourself from your thoughts and expectations. In this way, you are letting go of what you have been holding onto. Notice how this feels in your body and what new possibilities open up for you.

Let Go

35

Let Go

As you hold the old in place, so it will be.

Inquiry Practice

Call all your energy free, clear and pure, from blame, shame, guilt, anger, resentment and revenge. Call it from hopelessness, fear and self denial. Feel your Essence energy coming to you. Invite your younger ages and stages to be with you in the light of your heart space. Welcome them just as they are. Breathe into the unique light of your heart and welcome them home. Feel what you feel. Journal pearls of wisdom that are revealed.

Beverly Brunelle

Let Go of Judgment

Let Go of Judgment

36

Let Go of Judgment

Let Go. As you hold the old in place, so it will be.

Inquiry Practice

Are you willing to allow space for change to happen? Are you willing to be wrong in your assumptions? Are you willing to bring your attention away from judging the other, in order to find and feel a peace-filled place within yourself? Are you willing to be curious and open-minded? Explore this practice and notice how you feel.

Let Go of Perfection

37

Let Go of Perfection

Let go of the perfect way to respond in any given moment and let yourself come from deep within.

Inquiry Practice

Are you willing to allow something new to emerge from your inner wisdom? Are you willing to allow the movement of life to flow through you? Are you willing to be a little less perfect (in your own mind)? How would today be different if you lightened your grip on your ideals of perfection?

Beverly Brunelle

Let Your Light Emerge

38

Let Your Light Emerge

Don't get caught up in other's fantasies of life and how the world needs to be and how you need to express yourself. Don't get caught up in other people's lives and the tendencies of who they are, or who they think they are. Relax and let your light emerge more fully, that others may also share with you more fully who they are.

Inquiry Practice

Are you curious as to who you are becoming? Who your partner, child, family, friends are becoming? Are you willing to give space for yourself and for them to emerge in new ways? Experiment with this today and notice what happens.

Beverly Brunelle

Listening is the Key

39

Listening is the Key

It is an art to listen to yourself. Be curious and ask: What am I trying to tell myself? What do I need to hear from my very heart, soul, and Essence?

Inquiry Practice

Journal with these questions as your lead. Invite your consciousness to express what you haven't been able to hear, to know, to relate to, or to understand. Be willing to receive and reveal deeper knowledge about your unique self.

Beverly Brunelle

Look for Magic

40

Look for Magic

Anything is possible. Dare to dream your visions of what you want your world to be. Without effort or will, open to what presents itself. As you look for magic, it will manifest.

Inquiry Practice

As you go into a situation, relationship, meeting, etc., intend to look for magic. Invite the magic and let go of how it needs to appear. Allow yourself the freedom of being available to be surprised!

Beverly Brunelle

Love Beyond Imagination

41

Love Beyond Imagination

Love yourself beyond your imagination, expectations and dreams. Love yourself with your wounds, fears and doubts. Love all that you have judged about yourself and others. Rest in this marinade of Love.

Inquiry Practice

It takes no effort to love. Love is. Meditate and invite the highest frequencies of Love in to marinade your expectations, dreams, wounds, fears, doubts, judgments, and all your self-limiting perceptions. Breathe and relax into this field of Love. Without effort, notice insights, impressions, guidance, shifts and changes that are revealed. Give thanks to Love. Journal your pearls of wisdom.

Beverly Brunelle

Love Transforms

42

Love Transforms

What do you need? The answer is always Love. Feed yourself only Love. Let it just flow. Let go of despair, fear, judging, and all that makes you feel separate, different, left out, better than. Just be in love with the moment at hand. It will transform all those with you.

Inquiry Practice

Are you willing to explore being in more loving presence with yourself and the dynamics of the moment? Breathe into your heart space and rest there. Invite the highest frequencies of Love to open within you. Relax your mind and emotions and ask: "What are the origins of my concerns and judgments?" Experiment with this to discover how it shifts you and your relationship dynamics."

Beverly Brunelle

Love Yourself Well

43

Love Yourself Well

Stop the negative thinking about yourself and the dishonoring. It is time to love yourself well. Send blessings and love to the past that it may be recalled with loving compassion, valuing your existence, valuing the grace of your journey. Make not your origins wrong. Deny spirit within you no longer.

Inquiry Practice

Where are you denying spirit in yourself? In your relations? Work? Creativity? Perceptions of your past? Present? Future? Invite your inspired genius, your Essence, your magnificence, your radiance, and the highest frequencies of Love to shine more fully through you into your perceptions, actions, relations and life, now. Enjoy the organic changes that blossom forth.

Beverly Brunelle

No Boundaries in Reality

44

No Boundaries in Reality

You create the boundaries of your world. There is much to explore beyond your assumptions and conditioned expectations. You have the power to create new realities that bring great joy, creativity, nourishment, and love into life.

Inquiry Practice

Where do you feel stuck? Where have you felt you have no options? There are many worlds and endless possibilities beyond your normal ways of perceiving. Invite your Essence to show you new possibilities when you can't find any. Invite the magic of life and creation to inform you. Watch for the signs of inspiration that come.

Beverly Brunelle

No Situation is a Wall

45

No Situation is a Wall

No one else in your life is a wall. No opportunity or situation is a wall or an end or a stopping point, but only that which you judge it as. It is in truth, simply another doorway.

Inquiry Practice

Who or what are you perceiving as a wall or a block to your vibrancy, success, health, creativity, freedom, etc.? Journal these questions: "What new opportunity is this presenting for me? What will support me to see the doorway and to step through?"

Nurture Yourself

46

Nurture Yourself

Your thoughts and feelings have the power to deeply nurture you. Be aware and make choices that please, and perhaps even surprise you.

Inquiry Practice

Notice your thoughts. How do the thoughts about yourself and your life make you feel? Are they aligned with the reality you want to create and live in? Explore. Invite new, nourishing perceptions and possibilities that are outside your current and conditioned ways of thinking. Journal with an open mind and ask: What else is possible?

Beverly Brunelle

Open to New Possibilities

47

Open to New Possibilities

One can be buried in the past. Don't let this happen. Letting go of the past takes great courage. It takes a heart and soul of willingness, openness and curiosity. Structures have more to do with the past than the present. Honoring the past, undoing and dissolving the limiting structures of your past, allows you to open to new possibilities, new energies. It is the work of wonder.

Inquiry Practice

Ask: "I wonder what new possibilities are available beyond my past experiences and expectations?" Be curious about what is outside of your typical expectations, assumptions and experiences.

Open Your Heart to Receive

48

Open Your Heart to Receive

Let your heart be open to your Self. This is the source and a resource of clear communication, for the heart being open receives the gifts of life and pure creation.

Inquiry Practice

Breathe and bring your focus into your heart space. Rest your awareness there and relax your body, mind and emotions as you breathe. Invite the love in your heart space to reveal what you need to know at this time.

Beverly Brunelle

Override Yourself No More

49

Override Yourself No More

Trust your own loving presence. Bless your own needs and desires and be gentle in your own self-loving and nurturing. Truly honor that which is. Override it no more.

Inquiry Practice

Slow down. Be with yourself for five minutes. Notice your breathing, your thoughts, body sensations, and emotions. Tune into your deeper knowing and ask: "How can I be more loving to myself, today?" Journal your insights.

Beverly Brunelle

Passion is Your Guide

50

Passion is Your Guide

Passion is the fire that burns and creates peace within. You deserve all the passion, all the fire and all the peace. You deserve to love yourself. Pay attention to how you feel and take care of this tender one. Pay attention to the passions of the body. Pay attention to the passions of the heart. Let them be your guides.

Inquiry Practice

How is passion guiding you? Where are you blocking or ignoring its messages? How can you give passion more freedom to express in your life? Bring your awareness into your heart space. Breathe. Expand your awareness slowly throughout your entire body. Invite passion to communicate with you. What is passion wanting you to know? Send gratitude, and journal the pearls of wisdom you received.

Beverly Brunelle

Peace is Always Available

51

Peace is Always Available

Stop letting your thoughts run rampant like a spoiled child. Peace is available at all times. Be aware of the signs of your body and emotions. Be conscious in your choices. Nurture and support yourself with your thoughts and feelings. Find the feelings and thoughts that truly nurture and support you.

Inquiry Practice

Take charge of your thoughts. Be your own best parent and guide your self-talk to be more aligned with your radiant and loving Essence, your true nature, and your genius qualities.

Beverly Brunelle

Qualities are Within You

52

Qualities are Within You

Bring those qualities you see and admire in others and in your imaginings, to yourself. They are like dreaming and only represent that which is naturally in you.

Inquiry Practice

Dare to dream yourself beyond your conditioning. Dream yourself present, passionate, creative, valuable, sexy, successful, influential, loving, lovable, compassionate, and more. Play with enlivening these qualities in your daily experiences. Notice what is new in the days to come.

Beverly Brunelle

Radiate the Truth

53

Radiate the Truth

Trust your unique presence, creative spirit and deep wisdom. Radiate the truth of who you are from a level of knowingness. Others will respond to that.

Inquiry Practice

Breathe. Disentangle your energy from outside influences. Relax your awareness into your heart space. Invite your heart light to fill you and surround you. Notice the changes in your inner presence. Tap into and feel all the deliciousness that is uniquely you. Ask: "What supports me to radiate the truth of my being with greater ease?"

Beverly Brunelle

Respond from Your Awakened Heart

54

Respond from Your Awakened Heart

As new experiences present themselves, respond from your awakened heart.

Inquiry Practice

Be awake to new experiences. Tune into your heart space. Breathe. Communicate, make choices and take actions from your wise heart. Invite your creative Essence to inform and guide you.

Receive the Good

55

Receive the Good

Right now, be specific in your invitation and intention to receive the good, the abundance, the highest light that pure creation is flowing to you, around you, and through you. Relax and receive.

Inquiry Practice

Breathe and let go of tensions and expectations. Meditate like a flower opening to the morning sun. Invite the highest light. Be curious and ask: What good is here now that I have not been able to see? What sources of abundance are here for me, now? Invite clarity, insight, and wisdom, concerning your areas of interest. Listen deeply. Journal pearls of wisdom.

Beverly Brunelle

Share Like a Prayer

Share Like a Prayer

56

Share Like a Prayer

It is a delicate balance between the seen and the unseen. Your voice is vibrating. Share ideas and visions like a prayer, being in the true energy of adoration, respect and the mystery of its creation. This adds to the manifesting of it.

Inquiry Practice

Intend to be more aware of your choice of words and the future you are calling in. Make conscious changes in your speech and actions that are more in alignment with your highest desires. This will also influence your perceptions and expectations to create the realities you are truly wanting.

Self-Awareness is Key

57

Self-Awareness is Key

Before you can really and truly communicate with others, you need to know what is happening within yourself. Before you can truly listen to another human being, you need to be able to listen to yourself. To fully understand another human being, you need to truly and deeply understand yourself.

Inquiry Practice

Be willing to be more honest with yourself. What is deeply true for you? What is your inner wisdom and intuition wanting you to know? Are you accepting this or arguing with yourself? Journal your questions, and the flow of response that pours through, for deeper self-discovery.

Beverly Brunelle

Step into the Future

58

Step into the Future

Love yourself enough to acknowledge the past, to bring yourself into the present, and to step into the future you are wanting to create.

Inquiry Practice

Where are you still judging yourself for feeling guilty or angry for past choices and experiences? Call all of your energy from those times to you, now. Send love to all those ages and stages. Invite them home to your heart space. Listen deeply, with an open mind and heart. What do they want you to know, so that you may be more available to yourself, your current life choices, and to the future you are truly wanting?

Surrender to Unfolding

59

Surrender to Unfolding

Let go to the experience of yourself unfolding. Make nothing wrong. Just open to it. Allow yourself to be surprised.

Inquiry Practice

Be curious about yourself and who you are becoming. Experiment with your self expression and capacities to relate with others. Risk being seen with your authentic passions, strengths and creativity. Notice changes in your desires and needs. Explore your expanding perceptions of how you "hold" yourself.

Surrender to Your Magnificence

60

Surrender to Your Magnificence

Let go of the hardness of thoughts, the hardness of efforting and the confines of needing to know. Surrender to your magnificence and see yourself as part, a significant part, of the mystery of pure creation. This is a time of reconfiguration.

Inquiry Practice

Invite your magnificence to shine brighter through you. Relax, let go of expectations and be curious as to what is possible. Notice what's new: in your perceptions, organic expressions and authentic new behaviors. Be aware of your surroundings and notice what is calling for change.

Beverly Brunelle

Take Sacred Action

61

Take Sacred Action

Hold your space as sacred. Take action as sacred. Move from the spirit of joy within. Like begets like. Joy begets joy. Your mind sets results into an absolute form. Therefore, you create and manifest much tension and stress to perform. You come from predisposed ways. You know new ways. Join in with the energy of pure creation. Take action as a team. Call upon your future joy and success to guide you.

Inquiry Practice

Meditate and call upon your wise future self to provide insights and support for you taking sacred new action steps to create more joy and success in your life. You may want to ask your future selves what success means, and looks like, to them. Journal your discoveries. Experiment taking new sacred action with pure creation as your ally.

Beverly Brunelle

Thinking is an Art

62

Thinking is an Art

There is much wisdom and creativity within that is yet to be revealed. Let go into what arises from the heart. This is the essence of the art of thinking.

Inquiry Practice

Invite that which is beyond your typical ways of perceiving and responding. Befriend your deeper creativity and knowing. Be willing to explore the wisdom that rises from your heart.

Beverly Brunelle

The Magic of Creation

63

The Magic of Creation

Be clear, be specific, and be honest with what you need. The magic of creation will fill in the spaces.

Inquiry Practice

Risk being more honest with yourself. Meditate on your specific need. Open space around your mental and emotional expectations and invite magic to come in to inspire you. Journal your pearls of wisdom. Tune in regularly in meditation to continue to open space for magic to do its part.

The Magic of Fresh Possibilities

64

The Magic of Fresh Possibilities

To organize your thoughts around fear is to deny the existence and input of pure creation, of fresh possibilities, of love, and the magic of life itself.

Inquiry Practice

When you notice fearful thoughts, call all the energy you have invested in those thoughts and expectations home to your heart space. Breathe deeply and ask: What else is possible with the love and magic of life? Listen deeply and journal what ever comes to you. This can be a rich daily practice even when you aren't in fear.

Beverly Brunelle

The World is Very Malleable

65

The World is Very Malleable

Tap into the magic of the universe and the ability to create and recreate. The world is not as it appears to be. It is very malleable.

Inquiry Practice

Relax tensions in your mind. Lighten your grasp on what you think is absolute. Invite the magic of the universe to open and show you new possibilities in the areas of your concerns and interests.

Transformation is in Your Heart

66

Transformation is in Your Heart

The natural love in your heart is very powerful and ever present, even when you can't feel it. Anything you hold in your heart will be loved. You can let it go there.

Inquiry Practice

What or who are you judging? Take some deep breaths and bring your energy from these concerns into your heart space. Relax and feel into your heart space. Notice any shifts in your perceptions. What are you judging about yourself? Bring these into your heart space. Breathe, relax and notice what changes.

Beverly Brunelle

Tune into a Higher Vibration

67

Tune into a Higher Vibration

Divine flow presents itself in every moment. Watch the energies and feel the frequencies in existence. Every moment, you are repeating or rewriting, following or creating the program of your life. Tune into that which is a higher vibration than your daily fears and doubts.

Inquiry Practice

Notice when you are in automatic response mode. Stop. Make a conscious choice to be present in a higher vibration. Breathe and feel yourself align with the Divine flow within. Invite new possibilities and deeply listen within.

Beverly Brunelle

Understand Yourself First

68

Understand Yourself First

Take steps to understand yourself. *First*, ask yourself: What do I really feel? What do I really think in this moment? What do I really want? What is my intuition revealing? *Second*, be very curious, honest and receptive to what information and discoveries come into your awareness. *Third*, acknowledge it. Accept it. *Fourth*, ask more questions if you need to. *Fifth*, tune into how to best honor yourself. Always exercise your wise judgment about the appropriateness of taking any action. These steps are an exercise, first and foremost, in listening within and understanding yourself.

Inquiry Practice

Explore self-inquiry and deep listening as a regular practice. Remember to be curious, honest and receptive to what is revealed to you and to be discerning in your choices.

Value the Grace of Your Journey

69

Value the Grace of Your Journey

Send blessings and love to the past, that it may be recalled with loving compassion for yourself, valuing its existence and the grace of your journey.

Inquiry Practice

What specific experience, time in your life or age is wanting acknowledgement, loving compassion, and integration into the present moment? Meditate on this specific life experience. Invite the highest frequencies of Grace to infuse the situation. Welcome your younger self home to your heart space. Journal your insights.

Beverly Brunelle

Value Your Thoughts

70

Value Your Thoughts

Know your Self, your heart, your soul, your Essence. Come into and from these places within you. Nurture and value your thoughts as if they are pearls of your Essence going off into pure creation.

Inquiry Practice

Take space and time within your busy days to truly be with yourself and to honor the sacred being that you are. From this inner space, choose perceptions, thoughts, and words as sacred creations to express into life.

Beverly Brunelle

What Do You Need?

71

What Do You Need?

Stop judging other people and putting your energy in those directions. Bring your energy back home to yourself. Ask: "What am I needing in this moment?"

Inquiry Practice

Recall someone or a situation you have recently judged. Call all of your energy home to yourself free, clear, and pure—from the people and the situation. Inquire: "What did I actually need or want at that time?" With this new information, how could you have approached that situation more honestly? Is there something more appropriate to follow up with?

Beverly Brunelle

What are the Blessings of Right Now?

72

What are the Blessings of Right Now?

What blessings are in your life right now? With a deep breath, open your awareness to the goodness and new opportunities that are blossoming in and around you, right now.

Inquiry Practice

Create a gratitude journal. Keep it by your bed, in the kitchen, or in the bathroom. Make it easy to record in it daily to help you open your awareness. Look for qualities or behaviors within yourself and for very small and simple things to be grateful for. Notice the people and things you assume are always there for you. Have fun with being grateful.

Beverly Brunelle

What Do You Need to Let Go Of?

73

What Do You Need to Let Go Of?

The struggles that you experience in relationship can support you to become aware of and feel what you need to let go of. Things from the past, from the depths, have been stirred up for you to be aware of and to let them go. It's not always easy. Letting go allows you to step into a new space of inner and outer freedom, self-honesty and new possibilities.

Inquiry Practice

What do you really need, and what do you need to let go of? Journal for self-discovery: What challenges are you experiencing in your relationship with yourself and with those close to you? What do you really need? Has this theme been an issue in your life? What would set you free to perceive new possibilities to express yourself, to make new choices, and to freshen your relationships?

Beverly Brunelle

Welcome Your Essence

150

74

Welcome Your Essence

There is great ease and deep trust when one's own Essence comes through and is welcomed. To open up your creativity, honesty and magnificence is a gift to ALL. To give others space to truly be themselves and for you to find the truth that is within them, these are also great gifts.

Inquiry Practice

Are you willing to be curious about the mystery of the moment? Are you willing to let go of expectations and judgment of yourself and others, even if just for the time being? Experiment with being bold and step out of your comfort zone. How can you express more of your creative magnificence?

Your Presence is Important

75

Your Presence is Important

Act as if your heartfelt thoughts, feelings and expressions have influence and impact upon everyone you meet. Act as if your life this day is important, your presence is important, no matter where you are. Act as if creation is ready to open pathways to great success and abundance.

Inquiry Practice

How do humility and self-honesty support you in being more present? Review your past few conversations. When did you feel more authentic and real, and when were you efforting to match an ideal version of yourself or to meet another's expectations?

About the Author

Beverly Brunelle has been working and teaching in the fields of energy healing and human potential for over 30 years. She is an Intuitive and Master Energy Healer. Her passion is supporting people to shift from living limited beliefs, perspectives and expectations to dynamically awakening their authentic powers of freedom, clarity, creativity and purpose. Her work wakes up the personal fire of mysticism and higher intelligence in clients' lives.

Beverly facilitates individuals, couples and groups to create a new energy resonance within themselves and their past. This opens up fresh new possibilities for their current life and for living their most vibrant future.

To learn more about Beverly's work, or to contact her, visit **beverlybrunelle.com**.